For

~~educational purposes only~~
~~the benefit of the tape~~
~~the negligence claim~~
~~shits and giggles~~
~~future reference~~
~~the coroner~~
~~posterity~~
~~my~~ ~~Dad~~
you

Praise for

History of Present Complaint

◆

"*History of Present Complaint*' cleverly interweaves the terrifying past with the equally frightening present. HLR's debut is brave and raw as she stoutly refuses to shy away from the palatable. This collection of poetry and prose transgresses boundaries and will evoke a deep-seated grief and ache within any reader.

"*HLR's work focuses on dismantling the stigma surrounding psychosis in particular; her words are heartbreaking yet render an empowering and honest retelling of survival. There is pain embedded at every turn as her poetry and prose eviscerates both viscerally and vividly. The power is to be found in how HLR's courage and truth is an indictment of mental health care in the United Kingdom. The weaving of past and present crises honestly reveals how exhausting and traumatising survival and illness become in amongst the red tape, disbelief, shame and sheer unprofessionalism rife within the public health sector.*

"*The pieces within this collection combine brutal reality with stunning imagery to convey trauma, heartbreak and grief in a way which Plath's The Bell Jar never achieved. HLR steers a sturdy course and never romanticizes mental illness. Her purposeful imagery and structural formatting is not gratuitous, but explores the disassociation and obsession of a panicked mind, to reveal the frightening hold mental illness can have - as if being held hostage in your own body.*

"*Often, I wish to quote from poetry collections to allow just a tiny taster of what is to come, but 'History of Present Complaint' is a masterpiece to be read, savoured and experienced anew. This is not about spoilers but about preserving a collection in its startling and raw beauty. HLR is a marvel and I thank her for being here, for surviving, for continuing to draw breath and for courageously opening her* wounds for us in this collection. HLR does not deny the difficulty of living but neither does she deny the astounding beauty of living, and I salute this."

— **Kristiana Reed**, author of *Between the Trees* and *Flowers on the Wall*

"*After a while, when you've spent a lot of time reading poetry online, it's a damn challenge to find that which sticks. When it does, you know you've got a keeper. HLR could possibly be one of the most exciting poets of her generation, and yeah that sounds hackneyed but it's so close to the truth, it burns. I could easily wax lyrical here, and compare HLR to Plath, Bukowski, Childish, Sexton, or a raft of other notable poets you'd know the names of, but that's not going to cut it. HLR is a mysterious, slightly gorgeous, utterly deviant and exceptionally talented writer and I'd bet my horse on her any day. From my first encounter with her writing, I was addicted to her raw, brutal truth and the ability she has to write like nobody else I've read who is still living.*

"'*History of Present Complaint*' *is a collection of guttural cries from the unraveling depths of a human being who I happen to know is a really, really good human being, and it's a wonder she's still with us but a very, very good thing. This book is horrifying. Nothing less. I read it in one sitting (perfect length for a kick you in the mouth kind of read that leaves you sweating). This is written by someone who is more naturally gifted at writing than 99.9 percent of poets out there today. This isn't something you can forget and you'd better not try.*

"*I have read quite a few collections of 'my time in a psych unit' and this doesn't evoke any of them. It's a story written in blood, with very little distance between the actual moment of it happening and you reading the recollecting. If that doesn't make the hairs on the back of your neck rise, very little is going to. But like any macabre rendition, it's also desperately funny and horrifically detailed, guaranteed to dispel any notions of safety. HLR is an old soul for every one of her youthful years. She's actually completely hilarious too, as all very, very clever*

Contents

◆

people tend to be, she's got that sardonic wit down to a tee and it serves its bilious undertone very well against the horror of the psych ward.

We lament that art in its myriad of forms, is stale, lacking, aloof. And the purity of this collection is its lack of pretention, self-consciousness and formula. As if you had been there yourself. And there's a bloody lake of value to that because it's real, and it pulls you by the throat into the vortex that is trauma and refuses to politely lead you by the hand.

Should poetry be this visceral? Absolutely. Should women expose their experiences this blatantly? God yes. All that and more. All that and MORE. I want something real, don't you?

"'History of Present Complaint' is real. I wish it weren't. I really do. Because HLR went through this and that bothers me, a lot. But sometimes the ones who wanted to die the most, are the ones who can describe living the best: she got up and she wrote this and 'History of Present Complaint' is not all she is, by any measure, she's so much more, and you're going to see that in the coming years, I'm damn certain of it. In fact, I think I should say… I told you so."

— **Candice Louisa Daquin**, Senior Editor, *Indie Blu(e) Publishing*

FIRST CUT

History of Present Complaint

by
HLR

Close To The Bone Publishing

Editor's Note

One morning in late September 2019, you suffered an acute psychotic episode, during which you were detained under Section 135 of the Mental Health Act (1983).

In an attempt to make sense of what had happened to you, you spent the weeks after your release compiling a series of handwritten pages documenting your experience of the aforementioned psychotic episode, as well as its aftermath. You also produced retrospective accounts of psychiatric incidents of equal severity and significance that you had endured in previous years.

The pages were neither dated nor arranged in any specific order. For the sake of clarity, I have taken the liberty of classifying each article as being one of the following:

> *Present Complaint*
> > writing about the psychotic episode in September

> *History of Present Complaint*
> > recollections of previous psychiatric crises that occurred over the last decade

> *Post Complaint*
> > the immediate aftermath of the September episode

The following book consists of everything you wrote down in October 2019 – all that you could remember, and all that you couldn't forget.

Present Complaint //
There Were Five of Them

They asked you *what happened*, so you told them:

There were five strange men in your house. You had never met them /
seen them / spoken to them before. You were very scared but you were
also very brave. You fought those men with all of your might for seven
hours straight: the longest / hardest / toughest fight of your life. It was
brutal. They kept playing tricks on you / hiding in different places: in
cupboards / behind chairs / under beds / inside the tall bag of fishing
rods. They laughed when you couldn't find them. You so desperately
wanted them gone, you tried everything: shouting at them / trying to
make a compromise / reach a deal with them / violently attacking them
/ begging them / promising them money / sex / your silence. You didn't
know their names and you never saw their faces but you're able to
recount exactly what each of the five men looked like: height / build /
nationality / accent / hair colours and styles / clothing and footwear /
weapons / what their laughter sounded like / what they wanted to do
to   you   /   what   they   were   absolutely   *going   to*
do   to   you.

Then what happened? they asked:

The men refused to leave.
They hurt you.
They terrorised you.
They loved it.

Present Complaint //
Blues & Twos En Route

You thought that if you pretended to phone the police, they would:

    know you weren't messing around / apologise profusely / leave.

You made a mistake. A really, really big mistake. The biggest:

    you accidentally phoned the police for real.

"There are five strange men in the house, and they won't leave,"

    you shouted into the phone, loud enough for the men to hear.

"We're sending help now on blues and twos,"

    a voice replied from a slit in your shattered Samsung.

        "THEY'RE ALL EN ROUTE!" you announced to the house

        before locking yourself in the bathroom

        sitting down on the toilet seat lid

        smoking your last cigarette

        and realising, far too late,

        that the real danger

        was on its way.

History of Present Complaint //
Twenty-Five & Still Alive

You are 25 years old. Up early. Don't know what to wear. Late to meet him. Your shoulders are bare: very rare but it is a special occasion. London Bridge. Overpriced granola bar and a little panic. "We're going to have a lovely day," he says. Sudoku on the train. Broken biro. Not allowed to be sad, not now, not today. Today will be a lovely day.

Brighton. You never eat breakfast but have been informed that it is a requirement of 'a lovely day'. Vegetarian fry-up. No ashtrays. Hailstones, suddenly. Sarcophagus. Sunshine. Skeletons. Rain. Bright blue cocktails. *Blue is not a palatable colour*, you say, *that's why no food is blue*. Hear him thinking about blueberries; see the thought shoot out of his left ear.

Seaside. Arcade. Win a novelty keyring. Shingle. Football. The English Channel. Lose your left hoop earring. Revolting fishcake. Remember the text he sent you in January. Cry in gutter. "Don't be sad, baby, it's almost your birthday."

Nightclub. Want drugs. Have none. He won't dance with you. *Why won't you dance with me*? Argument. Flying beer. No fun. Angry cigarette. He disappears. Throw yourself into the path of fast cars but not fast enough. Man with a guitar serenades you, sings *Live Forever*, 'our song'. Dark-cold-late. Little girl running up big hill in big heels. Last train to London. Return home alone.

Lock the door. Heels off. Sit on kitchen floor. Bad song. Play the bad song again. Play it again. Spiral. *Why can't people just be nice*? Over[the-top]dose. 1... 2... 34... 56 pills / nom / pink ones / nom nom / blue ones / nom nom nom. Choke down all those lovely little heartstoppers with warm white wine. Broken glass. Hot skin. Air, please, and no more songs. Must get out. *Can't be here.* Too hot. Need air.

Down the mildewed staircase. Crash through fire escape. Outside. An adventure! *A birthday adventure.* Past overflowing bins. Through car park. Outside fancy Italian furniture shop. Cold concrete pavement. That is so nice. Sandbag as a pillow. *This is so nice.* Finally: time for that sweet forever-sleep.

But noise. Footsteps. Men everywhere. Touching you. Grabbing you. Above you over you by you next to you they want to get inside of you. *I am not safe.* You are not safe.

Get the fuck away from me

BLACKOUT

Ambulance.

—Hello, can you tell me what you've taken?

BLACKOUT

—She's in hypothermic shock

BLACKOUT

(?)

BLACKOUT

Wake up to find a lady trying to prise the silver rings off your fingers. What the fuck is this? Confusion. *I'm...* not dead? Shock. *I'm not dead.* A ward. A ward like all the wards before. Lights leads beds.

You're not dead and you know that it is not a good idea to be alive in a hospital. Adrenaline. Fight or flight. While you decide, the lady disappears, draws the paper curtain behind her. Fight. No. Flight. No. BOTH. Must get out. Must get outside. Need a cigarette. Need to be anywhere else but here. Need to go. Away.

Hard to walk. Shit. Woah no balance. No balance at all. Do not fall on the floor. Lockjaw. Pins and needles [are the same thing]. You need to fucking walk. Get out of here, get away, get home, go straight to the bus stop, you know where it is, you just have to fucking get there. Now. And quickly. Come on. Slip through ward door. Good, this is good, keep walking away away away.

Followed. Cornered. An unknown force holds your wrists in a death grip. Hands. That belong to a police officer. He drags you into a small room off the corridor.

Help, help, hELP ME HELP HELP

—Nobody is coming to help you

> Get off me or I'll scream

—No point shouting, love, no one can hear you. It's just you and me now

> Don't you fucking touch me please get away from me you can't do this

—Ha! You can't call the police on the police!

> HELP ME PLEASE SOMEONE HE'S HURTING ME

—Who would they believe? Me, a respected copper, or you, a mad, drunk slut?

Get the fuck off me please get off me

Call for backup. Lots of people grabbing you. Men men men everywhere, on you, a thousand hands on you, on your skin, your tiny body. Hit police officer in the face (apparently).

BLACKOUT

Wake up. Scared of policeman. Nurse says, "some people are actually unwell and need your bed." Agree with nurse. Apologise for taking up their time. Try to leave. *No, you've made a mistake, you can't actually keep me here. The nurse told me to leave. Yes, I'm leaving now. Thanks. No, I'm going home. What the fuck are you doing, get off me*?! Staff swarm. Dragged back.

Cigs and lighter have disappeared. Phone is dead. Keys are missing. *This is ridiculous.* Time to leave. *I need a cigarette.* Try to leave. Followed by uniformed strangers. They mispronounce your name. *I am leaving. You can't keep me here, you know. I know my rights. I'm going home.*

Dark-blurry-cold. *Stay the fuck away from me.* Hard to walk. Wobbly walk. Do not trip over the kerb. You're not drunk, just sad. And alive. Reach bus stop. *I'm free?* You're free. *Now, where's a bus when you need one?* Both of your arms grabbed from behind by someone with A4-sized hands. A man. A big man with A4 hands and arms the width of your hips.

Dragged 400 yards by monster security guards. Kicking and screaming. *You have no right to keep me here. Get off! Let me go. Why are you doing this to me? You have no right. You're hurting me. Please stop hurting me. You have no right.* Passer-by doesn't help you. Passer-by doesn't stand up for you. Passer-by videos the scene on their phone. Hospital corridor. Automatic doors shut. A metal clunk.

8

Quiet. Everything is quiet for a precious moment and you think that now you actually *are* dead.

There's nobody around but you and the bastard security bully boys and the policeman who called you a slut. They are three times your size. Big bastard men. Brick shithouses. Hands everywhere. Grabbing at your bare breasts. *Get off me.* T-shirt ripped. The sound of your wrist cracking. *Please get off me.* A shove. Lying on floor. Can't move. *Please.* Cold floor on your cheek. Hear them mispronouncing your name again again again. Shouting at you. A man bellows "GET UP!" His spit is on your face. You cannot move to wipe it off. Someone kicks you in the back. No scream left in you. Blink. No words left. Blink. Blink.

BLACKOUT

Wake up in CT scanner. Head hurts. Raise hand to back of your head. Someone shouts at you from the other room, "Stop moving." Blood on your fingers.

BLACKOUT

—We tried to help you, but you moved in the scanner so it's your own fault

What is? What's my fault?

BLACKOUT

Wake up in the same bed as before. *I'm leaving. You scumbags hurt me. Look. Look! Look at what you did to me. You have no right. I'm not under section. I know my rights. You can't keep me here.* Security and police form a human wall to keep you in the unit. *You fucking bastards. Why are you doing this to me? Why?* You give up. Cry. Hide under bed.

9

—For fuck's sake, will you stop messing around?

Quietly tie an electrical cable around your neck.

—She's a bloody nightmare, this one

Handcuffed to the bed. Wrist feels broken; the skin has gone green.

You can't do this you can't do this you can't do this

—Shut up, you're putting me off my game

Sob and sob and sob. Wish they'd killed you.

Please phone my brother. Brother's phone is broken. *Try again. Please.*
"No." You only know one other phone number. You don't want to
but you have to. You have no other choice.

Please phone my mother. Mother is at work. Mother is furious. You
give up. *I will never get out of here alive. Wish I'd died at home.* Why
did you decide to go outside? *It was hot inside, I was too hot, I had to
go outside to turn into ice.*

Mother arrives. Mother arrives! A miracle. You are terrified of her yet
you have never been so relieved to see her in all your life. You tell her
they hurt you. Mother is not on your side.

I need you on my side. Get me out of here. I'm begging
you. Please

—Clean yourself up, you look a mess

I smell disgusting

10

—Don't worry, I have no sense of smell anymore

Please get me out of here, please

Mother speaks with one of the evil nurses. She finds your keys. She says some words and then you both walk out of the unit. Just like that. Out of the ward. You leave. Down the corridor. You slurp water straight from the nozzle on the communal dispenser. You can barely stand. You are outside. She saved you. Mother saved you. You're free.

You saved me. You saved me. Thank you

—I can't look after you

I know. Mum, they hurt me

—I know

They wouldn't give me water or let me go to the toilet. My head hurts

—Mhmm

Thank you for saving me

—Well. Goodbye

Bye, Mum.

Home. Traumatised. Wish you'd died. Empty pill packets crunch under feet. Turn phone on. Nobody. Nothing. No message from him. Panic attack(s). Climb into bath. Too weak to wash. Bloody / bruised / broken / bed. Nightmares of the bully boys. And hands on you. And the copper: his face, a young Tony Adams, hair like feathers. You are full of sharp edges and fear and you wish that you'd died.

11

...

Wake up to the sound of your own screams. You are 26 years old. Injuries are bad. They really hurt you. No messages wishing you a happy birthday. On your 15th birthday, over 600 friends and family wished you a happy birthday. Today: nothing and nobody. Not even Domino's pizza. *Fuck them.* Phone your care-coordinator, trembling.

—I was just reading the report...

They hurt me

—I know

They had no right. Was I under section?

—Ermmm, not according to this, no...

Not even section 5 holding?

—No

So them stopping me from leaving...?

—Was against the law

Against the law

—Yes

I knew it

—I'm sorry they did that to you

I never saw a doctor

—I know

I never had an assessment

—I know

I never saw a member of the mental health team even for a
second

—I know

They punished me, they hurt me, they fucked me up, they
properly fucked me up

—I know

I will never come back from this

—Don't say that

It's true. I will never come back from this. If, with the
benefit of hindsight, I had the choice between dying in the
street of hypothermia and poisoning, and those 12 hours in
hospital, I'd choose the former, without a doubt. They really
hurt me

—I know, I'm so sorry

They were supposed to help me. They were supposed to
keep me safe. They did the opposite. They had no right

—I'm so sorry

13

I'll never come back from this

—I'm sorry

Me too

Me too.

Present Complaint //
Overkill

4 cop cars / 2 riot vans / a meat wagon
kicked the door down / stormed upstairs / searched the house

there were too many
men in the house so
many men too man-
y men too many [police]men
around you 10 / 12 / 15 coppers
surrounding you and they told you that they

       "could not locate the assailants anywhere in the property"

they trapped you in a room they were big
they were huge in hats and belts and you are so tiny
tiny tiny little girl in your vest and knickers

       "we can't find them anywhere"

you explained calmly that they'd obviously run away
they ran when they heard the sirens / saw the lights

       "there was never any men 'ere, was there?"

they just didn't look properly did they did try the attic?
they should check the garage / the bushes / the bins

       "these men never existed, did they?"

OF COURSETHEYEXISTYOU SAW THEMTHEYWEREHERE

15

"no you didn't"

THEREWERE FIVEOFTHEMYOUSAWTHEMHERE

"there are NO men"

YOUFUCKINGNSAWTHEM FORGODSSAKETHEYHURTYOU

"right, I've had enough of this, let's get 'er out of 'ere"

Present Complaint //
Left You There To Rot

They said that you lied.

That you are liar. But,

truthfully,

they were the liars

there were men and they failed to catch them so they pretended there were none because they didn't want to admit they failed to keep you safe they were supposed to keep you safe but they failed they failed so they lied and called you a liar and they shouted at you and looked at you in a bad way and confiscated your Daddy's penknife and dragged you outside and cuffed you in the street and made a big scene and then they sectioned you even though you begged them not to and they didn't listen to you didn't listen to a word you said they were horrible to you and didn't keep you safe and let the bad men escape and they just laughed at you and called you a liar and threw you in an ambulance and took you to the hospital where you and your brother were born and then they took away the glass and the frame that held the photo of your Daddy the photo that was the only thing you managed to keep on you and then they locked you in a padded room and left you

they left you

they left you

they left you there to rot.

History of Present Complaint //
Twenty-One & On The Run

Accidentally overdosed—*honestly, it was an accident*—a purposeful accident, if you will, like, accidentally-on-purpose, yes, but an accident nonetheless.

You remember going downstairs / out through the front door / speaking to a man at the side of the road—*Gerry*? *Gary*? The desire: to lie down on cold concrete. The dream: to sleep for England. Then: nothing at all.

BLACKOUT

Wake up in a hospital. Bed. Ward. Harsh lights. Ugly gown. IV drip. Standard set up. Usual scene: too bright / everything hurts / you don't understand anything. Two nurses speaking in tongues by your bedside. You have to find your own tongue and use it.

     What is happening?

—Ah, helloooo! She's waking up now, good, good

     What the fuck is this?

—Hello, hello, you've been unconscious for some time, darling

     What? How?

—But you're in the hospital and we've been looking after you

     What?

—You just stay still and I'll call a doctor

    No, what? No

—Hey, hey, hey, this mask stays *on* and just keep your arms *there* for me, there, that's good

    I have to go home

—Are you hungry? You should eat something, little lady

    No, no, I need to go now

BLACKOUT

Wake up to a nurse trying to spoon-feed custard into your closed mouth.

    What is happening?

—Just try to stay still

    No, no, no, no

—You have to wait for someone from the mental health team to see you but it's going to take a while and you need to stay conscious long enough to sit and talk to them, okay?

    No, thanks, no, I'm fine, really, I'd like to go home now please

—You have to stay here. You've hurt your head and your body is very poorly right now

    No, I'm fine, thank you, thanks though, I need to phone my

Dad and check he's okay, where's my phone?

—I don't know, darling, is this your bag?

Yes, that is my bag, where's my phone?

—Ummm… there's no phone in here

Where's my stuff?

—This is all you turned up with

What? How did I get here?

—Ambulance I guess, darling, you were on a different ward before you came here

Oh, what? Fuck. Is it very early morning? Or just morning?

—No it's dinnertime, coming up to 8 o'clock now

On… Wednesday?

—Nooo, it's Friday night!

You are fucking joking me

—Hey! There's no need for that language

I'm so confused. I don't like this. Oh my God

—Just try to relax, please, come on

I need my meds now if it's dinnertime

—No, absolutely not, no more medication for you

> No, you don't understand, I need my meds. I'm on lithium.
> I need it now. Lithium and all the rest, please, I have to take
> them now otherwise I'll get sick, please. Withdrawal
> symptoms start straightaway if I don't take them on time
> and it's so horrible and I get so sick so quickly, please, I
> have to take them at the same time every day or else I get so
> ill, it's so important that I have them now, you don't
> understand, please

—No, we can't do that

> But I need them

—Well, you'll have to wait until you're stable and you've seen the
psychiatrist and been assessed, then we'll see what the doctor decides
when he does his rounds later tonight

> No, please. I need them now. I'll get so sick without them,
> please

—Just stay there, I'll try to find a doctor. And keep the oxygen mask
on

10 minutes drifting in and out. *I have to leave.* You have to go home
and get your meds. Where is your phone? The security guards finish
their shift at 8pm. Must leave before new guards arrive. Limited time
frame. *I'm on a mission from God.* Think of The Blues Brothers.
Laugh. "Everybody needs somebody to love." Suddenly remember
that Daddy's dead. Fight back tears. *Pull yourself together, for god's
sake.* This is neither the time nor the place for grief. You need to
leave. Now.

Mask off. Disconnect wires. Gown off. T-shirt on. Shoes on.

Sunglasses on. Grab bag. Get up off the bed. Wobbly woaaahhh woah woah shaky baby, shaky. *Fucking get a grip, you have to get out of here.* Try to walk in straight line past nurses' station. Through the double doors. Turn the corner. Run.

Hide in the toilets. Wash face. Peel off all plasters / bandages / visible ECG electrodes. Rip off I.D band with teeth. Wash off blood and smudged make-up. Try to look like a passable human being. "Smile! You're on camera." Run.

Realise that you've successfully absconded without being chased by security or stopped by police. You've only gone and done it! *I've bloody gone and done it*!

BLACKOUT

Wake up on bathroom floor. Grab meds. Find a note in your letterbox saying "Feel better xx" in unfamiliar handwriting. Panic. Get to a bus stop. [This bit is hazy]. Wake up on his doorstep. Ring doorbell over and over and over and ov—

Do you have my phone?

—Oh my God, you're alive! No, I don't have your phone, what the hell happened, we were so worried?!

I don't know what happened

—Come here

He hugs your whole body and even though the hug is full of love, it hurts.

Please can you help me?

—Of course. You're safe now, my darling

      Can you please get all these fucking ECG stickers off me? I
      think I missed some

—Yeah, let me have a look at you

      Just get it all off me, I don't want it

Burst into tears.

—You're safe now, babes

      Thank you

—I'll put the kettle on

      Thank you

—Hang on, what's that?

Oh, shit. Another cannula. Wire-like tubes dangling out of your arm.
Rip it all out. The plaster pulls a layer of skin off with it. Fuck it.
Shower. The shower hurts and the water goes right through your flesh
and hits your bones, the stream of water tapping your skeleton like
Morse code dot dot dot dot dot all dots no dashes all dots. See
yourself in the mirror and look like Death warmed up.

      I'm so tired

—What happened?

      I don't know

—You don't have your phone?

No, I thought you had it

—No, I don't

Fuck. That was my Dad's phone as well, it had all his
photos and contacts and old text messages on it

—Shit, don't worry, we'll look for it, baby. Maybe the hospital has it?

Doubt it

—Wait, so you ran away whilst on psych watch and you've lost your
phone... they're going to go to your house, you know. They'll be
looking for you

I just want to sleep, I'm so tired, baby

SLEEP

Something bad happened in Barcelona, didn't it?

—I don't think I should tell you about that right now

SLEEP

—Brucie's dead

I thought he died ages ago

—Nah, you're thinking of Terry Wogan

SLEEP

Your favourite pizza. Meds. Your favourite person. Try to stay awake.

I'm safe. You think, *I think I'm safe.*

I don't think I should drink champagne

—You don't have to, I'm just celebrating the fact that you're alive

Just about

—Just about. And it is Friday night after all!

SLEEP

I need to sleep for a while. I need to sleep for a week. I'm so tired. I'm sorry

—I love you

SLEEP

Present Complaint //
With Your Eyes

There *were* men because you saw them you saw them with your eyes apparently you lied and the men weren't real but they were real they were real they *were* real you saw them they hurt you the men hurt you they terrorised you you saw them with your own eyes they terrorised you and they loved it and you saw them do it and they hurt you you saw it with your own eyes all of them all of the men that's what men do that's what men do to you they hurt you all of the men hurt you.

It was real. It was real. It was real to you.

History of Present Complaint //
Sixteen & Psychotic

North London, Edmonton, on a Tuesday afternoon—you are sixteen and psychotic and should be at school—you don't know what you're looking for but it probably definitely has to be here, in this huge supermarket so grip the sticky handles of that blue plastic basket and LOOK! your name! your name is on the front page of every single one of   those   newspapers!
  NO don't look at them   look *sane* okay???   look SANE look
sane   look   sane   look   sane   looksanesaeseanesnaes

grocery shopping is good—it's what humans do—it's a good thing to do—sensible, good—look at you! you are so good—they sell everything here! those tulips are expensive, you imagine—push your shredded thumbs through the crust of warm golden loaves—the doughy interior burns ouch! how unpleasant, you say aloud and the bakery boy frowns—but you know what to do, of course you do! you are a little genius—the frozen aisle awaits, all that cold goodness, all that coldness, it is waiting for you, it exists for you, it is nice to be cool, you think—cool to be nice, you think too—nice nice baby—but no oh my god oh my god no there's not enough room in the chest freezer to fit you—begin to remove the boxes of chicken nuggets and fish fingers but the shelving is stuck fast—the freezers will not accommodate you this time, there is no space for your bad brain and burnt thumbs and too-short school skirt which is such a shame, you say, such a crying shame: you only   wanted   to   be   cool

look around you—find an old lady's pinched face staring, glaring into yours—pinched and confused—yes, confused, and so are you—you are neither sensible nor good nor cold—standing by a pyramid display of red wine—racks upon racks of red and shiny silver badness in your head —grab a neck from the bottom row of bottles—you must deliver it like a baby—it wants to be saved, it has to be saved, it has to be saved by   you—and   then   suddenly the   Red   Sea

the crash of collapse the smashed sand the flood of juice and blood painting your feet staining the floor that was dirty already a shriek! a shriek escapes from the ancient lady's pinched face you are barefoot bloody pinch the source of the shriek bloody wine security man shouts no words mouth shouts but no sound no sound comes out and you cannot drown: you are not allowed you are not allowed to drown today you   must   carry   the   baby   and   swim   away,   swim   far   away and   out   out   out   out   out-

-side in the loading dock the gate is locked—remember when your skirt got caught? when he loved you? that was not so long ago—you should be at school but you have nothing no one nowhere to go no shoes no home no fear but blood and guts and glass glass in your soles and tiny toes and holes in your heart and an orange in your jacket pocket and a   baby   in   your   bloody   arms

Present Complaint //
Whatever Her Name Is, She's Wrong

A mental health nurse named Clare / Cathy / Carla
informs you that your whole psychotic episode,

from its initial presentation
until the moment the police arrived,

lasted less than 40 minutes.
Clara / Carol / Carly is wrong.

You fought the men for 7 hours straight.
And you have the bruises to prove it.

Post Complaint //
Fuck F***

He counted your bruises—fifty-five—and you cried
because you hate the number five; three and seven
and nine are fine, but not five, no, never five

> the number is unlucky to you
> your birthday is the 15th
> and it makes you sick

> f*ve

> look at you, how it pains you to write it

> FIVE – FIE. V. — FY. Vuh. — Fiiiv.

> shudder

> it isn't a nice number
> it isn't nice in any voice / type / colour

> and, also, it doesn't look nice as a shape
> on a page or the bathroom scales or etched
> and filled with gritty gold paint on the marble
> that sits atop the as-yet-unsettled grave

> 555555

> ouch

it cuts you with the point of its
sharp hat and its soft curve is
deceptive / it does not hug
it digs / into your ribs
and it hurts

fuck f***

He placed his warm palm over the dandelion disc
that was blooming on your thigh and laid his weathered lips
upon the swollen merlot shiner surrounding your right eye:
for you, he made it fifty-three, but you didn't deserve any.

Present Complaint //
This Is Your Life Now

There is something about being in hospitals that makes you feel disgusting. Maybe it's the:

dirty handprints on the wall / bloody cannula on the floor / sticky plastic mattress / smell of piss / torn-up tissues / stranger's identification wristband / words WHY and HELP scratched onto the unopenable chicken-wired opaque window / broken soap dispenser in the toilet* / cameras in the top corners of the "room" with their incessantly blinking red lights / stupid electronic calendar above the guarded door that says

THURSDAY

EVENING

18:12 PM

26TH SEPTEMBER 2019

26/09/19

You watch it change** from morning to evening to morning to evening to morning because this is your life now and they will never let you out.

---

* You couldn't pee even though you really needed to because they were there, watching you

** But you do not trust it because you know that it's really 13th April 2021

History of Present Complaint //
Custody Conversations

1 /

Copper 1:	How's she doing in there?
Copper 2:	Oh Christ, she's fitting
You:	Need meds pleaseneed mymeds
Copper 2:	Hold her legs
You:	Pleasmmmymmmeds needmedsmmedmed
Copper 1:	I'll call a doctor
You:	mmmedsdmdmds
Copper 2:	Stay still
Copper 1:	He'll be here in a moment

The doctor never came, the meds went untaken
the seizures seized in you until you seized no more.

Later, you came to, frozen and drenched in sweat,
alone on the dirty floor, your lips bitten to ribbons.
You left without ever having seen a medic.

You:	That's a strangely designed chair...
Support Worker:	Yeah, it's called a Rhino chair
You:	Why 'Rhino'?
SW:	Well, it's filled with sand so it's extremely heavy

You watch her struggle to drag the chair through the doorway. She puts her clipboard / phone / pens / bottle of Fanta on the floor and tries again using both hands. She bends her knees and heaves, and you see her orange underwear peep out over the band of her jeans.

SW:	It's supposed to make the chairs harder to throw
You:	Right...
SW:	People still manage to throw these chairs around though. You'd be surprised!!
You:	No, I really wouldn't

You would not be surprised. She gives up trying to move the Rhino and leaves to source a chair from elsewhere. You get up off the plastic mattress and drag the Rhino into the centre of the cell. When she returns, wheeling in a spinning desk chair, the support worker is surprised to see you sitting there.

You do not like surprises...
and, apparently, neither does she.

SW:	How'd you do that?!
You:	My friend moved it for me
SW:	Your friend?
You:	Yeah, my friend, John

She looks around the cell. You are the only two people in it.

| SW: | And where is... John now? |

You: What do you mean? He's sitting right there!

You point to the unoccupied mattress. The support worker is horrified.

You: Oh my god, I'm fucking JOKING!

You laugh your head off.

You: Jeeeesus, your face!!!

Apparently, she doesn't like jokes either. She leaves. The door locks behind her.

You spin on the desk chair for minutes or hours.
Later, when someone brings you a strawberry yoghurt,
you get in trouble for having the spinny chair and it gets wheeled away.
You have no idea of the time but imagine that it's dark outside.
You were not provided with a spoon.

John: I wouldn't eat that if I were you
You: Why not?
John: It expired eight months ago

You check the date on the lid.

John: Told ya.

You sit on the Rhino chair and cry. John drinks your yoghurt like a tequila slammer.

Doctor:	So it says here, you took sixteen tablets, is that right?
You:	No, sixty
Doctor:	Sixteen?
You:	Six-TY
Doctor:	Sixty?
You:	Yes, sixty
Doctor:	Sixteen?
You:	SIXTY
Doctor:	Look, if you're not going to co-operate with us…

Later, when you read the report, they said you'd taken six:
less paperwork for them, less time inside for you
which you appreciated, though your liver did not.
Your next ECG is a shitshow and bloodwork proves
your kidneys to be furious too, but everyone knows
that it's better to have your organs slowly fail you
in the relative safety of your own home.

Present Complaint //
Means of Escape

THE PLAN /

You know how this works. You've done this before. You know that there's only one way to make it out of here alive: you must tell them *exactly* what they want to hear, no more and no less. And you *must* be convincing. You have no choice, no fight, no flight. You know the script, now you must recite it verbatim. You must give the performance of your life. Either that or stay in this cell and die. Your critics await.

THE ASSESSMENT /

"No, *of course* I don't have any plans to end my life! I'm not psychotic *at all*, obviously my drink must have been spiked or something. I'm absolutely *fine*, it was just a one-off moment of madness. I mean, I haven't had a psychotic episode in *years*, seriously, like, *a decade* or something. I have no idea why it's happened now, I think I must have just smoked a dodgy rollup without realising hahaha honestly, to tell you the truth, I'm pretty embarrassed about the whole thing... I can't wait to get home, have a shower and get back to *normal* life! But thanks *so* much for everything, you guys have been *really* great."

THE VERDICT /

They bought it. Your Sanity Speech, your silly soliloquy:
they bought it. They ate it up. They believed you.
They fucking believed you.*

They checked their watches and ticked their boxes and thought about
what to get from the canteen for dinner and signed their forms and
made you promise not to kill anyone and said that they hoped they
wouldn't see you ever again and then they let you go.

Just like that. As if nothing had ever happened.

Well, you suppose, to them, nothing *did* happen.

THE AWARD /

for Best Actress goes to…

You! *You.* The madwoman. The criminal. The liar.

THE TRUTH /

You are not a liar but you had to tell lies this time because you had no
other choice and it worked to your advantage and you still have your
truth, you still have your truth inside you, an ancient mosquito
trapped in the black rock of your heart. You'll need a sledgehammer
to get to your truth, but it's there, it's in there, it's in there and it's
yours.

---

* They did not believe you when you told them that one of the men was lying
  underneath the bed, licking your bras, sniffing your underwear, but they believed
  you when you said you were fine

Present Complaint //
Sweet Release

You have never been so relieved
to breathe in pollution, to find your feet
standing on concrete at the bottom of Highgate Hill.

You got out. You lied your way out of the padded room,
and now you stand, outside, alive, a sobbing Sisyphus
with holes in your socks and shakes in your veins.

You feel fizzy

       [when you were 18, you burnt your fingertips off]

Your body is fizzing under its skin

       [in all of your dreams, he is in trouble]

You spilled everything and you're *still* not empty

       [on your 21st birthday, you set your hair on fire]

Psht <<< that's the sound of a can opening

       [you wore black to his wedding, red to his funeral]

North London has never looked so _____.

You are not okay but   you are not inside

You feel fizzy inside but   you are outside

You are outside so   you are free

You are free and   you *are*

you   are

you

are

you

are

you*

---

*   are not a liar

Post Complaint //
Community Spirit

You are released from hospital and returned into the "care of the community."

Your community consists of an awful Wetherspoons pub and the old men who drink in it; friends of your dead Daddy's who promised him before he left that they'd keep an eye on you.

You are anxious to go to the pub. Your brother tells you: it's fine / it will be fine / you'll be absolutely fine.

You do not feel fine. You do not feel fine after a glass of wine or a bottle of wine / several double vodkas / four tequilas.

You should've eaten and taken your meds hours ago but you chose alcohol over nourishment, not for the first time.

You leave the pub alone, without saying goodbye, hide under the railway bridge, and cry like you've never cried before: no tears come out.

You enter the £1 pizza shop and cringe under the cruel fluorescent lighting. You order the veggie special even though you hate mushrooms.

You are too dead inside to tell the pizza guy otherwise: it just seems too tiring to explain to him why you're averse to fungi. You tell yourself, "there's just no time."

You decide that, while you wait, you should go into the other pub, the pub across the road / that's full of trouble / from which you are barred.

This is a terrible idea.

In the smoking area you confront a man who hurt you in January: a man whose lies about you destroyed your relationship, whose lies caused a good guy, a good man whom you thought was the love of your life, to send you a text message telling you to die.

You are drunk. You shouldn't be here. You shout at him but he's "not scared of you." You receive no apology.

You call him a prick. You knock back your whisky and do not wince. You tell him he's a fucking dead man.

You storm out.

You run all the way home.

You forget to collect your pizza.

History of Present Complaint //
Twenty-Two & Dissociating

He found you lying on the floor underneath the bus stop bench. He crouched down, put his face parallel to yours on the ground, and said your name over and over again; each syllable felt like a piece of gravel falling on you, hundreds of little stones with your name written on them were crashing all about you; it was raining grains of grit and you felt them dully pinging off your skin.

He was there and you were there but you're not sure where. Your outer body was convulsing—your hair / teeth / nails / juddering violently—but inside you were immotile Medusan stone. Deathly still. But he couldn't see that. He could only see that you were shaking more than usual and that your eyes were full of cloudy tears, and then you both heard your voice crack as you whispered, "I don't know where I am."

You were terrified but he was terrified-er. He scooped you up and carried you to his car, wherever it was, wherever you were, whoever you were. He put your seatbelt on for you; you told him (firmly or in a whisper or in your head) not to bother. He locked the doors and said, "It's my job to keep you safe." As the two of you drove down roads you'd never seen before, you were still but your eyes were running without your permission. You couldn't move your legs. You had concrete set in your veins and anchors for shoes. You couldn't speak, but that was fine because you didn't know any words.

Later, you found yourself at his house, tucked up on the sofa in your usual corner, wearing his big, comfy clothes, with *Only Fools and Horses* on television and a pint of water on the table next to you. He was cooking Sunday dinner. You could hear him stirring gravy in the glass jug.

You dragged myself to the kitchen and stood in the doorway. He was startled when he turned around and saw you there. You quietly asked him what had happened. He said he didn't know. You started to panic. You both sat down on the sofa and he told you that:

You had called to tell him that you

- were just leaving home
- were going to buy some smokes from Bossman's
- would meet him at the £1 pizza shop in 10 minutes
- were putting pineapple on your half of the pizza
- didn't give a shit about his fruit-can't-be-a-topping argument because tomato

Then you texted him to say that you

- didn't feel good
- didn't feel very good
- *really* wasn't feeling very good at all
- couldn't walk
- couldn't walk anymore
- couldn't walk anywhere anymore
- needed to sit down
- weren't on this planet
- weren't in your body
- weren't anywhere
- were nowhere

You didn't show up at the pizza place and wasn't answering your phone. He went to the shop and Bossman told him that you *had* been in earlier, "acting like weirdo" and then you'd stumbled out. So he walked around the area looking for you and then he found you at the bus stop (the bus stop by your flat / Bossman's shop / your old school / the Tube station that you use every day).

When he found you, you were really frightened because you didn't know where you were / who you were / who he was / what was happening. You were screaming into your wrists and wouldn't move. It took 25 minutes for himself, three passers-by and an off-duty nurse to persuade you to trust him enough to let him grab you from underneath the bench and pick you up.

He told you that the girl he found underneath the bus stop bench

- wasn't you
- was someone else entirely
- was like an alien or a ghost or an orphaned infant
- had totally blank, soulless eyes
- didn't recognise his face at all
- didn't seem to understand what humans were
- had no idea where she was

He said that it was as if you were seeing the area that you've known like the back of your hand for over 20 years for the first time. You were scared of the buses / people / cars / air / pavement / sounds and your own heartbeat / skin / voice / existence.

He said that he had never seen anything like it in his entire life. He thought that

- perhaps you'd overdosed (on crack? spice?? meth???)
- perhaps you were possessed by a demon
- you were going to die
- you might kill someone
- you might kill him

He had wanted to call an ambulance but he knew that being in hospital would terrify you more and make you worse. He said that he'll never forget the state he'd found you in, and that while he's

45

"quite frankly, terrified" of you, he would always do whatever it takes to help you be the "normal, non-possessed" girl that he knows and loves.

Apart from a minute in a car, you couldn't remember a single thing. You didn't know what was real or right or wrong or true. You just didn't know.

"Look," he said, and pulled your sleeves up. Bloody great bite marks on your wrists / the back of your right hand / your forearms, all red / purple / violent / frantic, punctures in your flesh that fit your teeth.

You looked up at him and his eyes were soft and safe, like golden syrup. You knew then that you could always find asylum in the irides of his eyes.

"I'm scared of me too," you said.

He hugged you, being careful not to hurt you, and then mumbled into your hair, "Do you want one Yorkshire pudding, or two?" and you laughed and cried into his chest, unable and unwilling to make sense of anything in that moment other than that one question.

"One and a half, please," you replied.

He had no idea then that, one day, he will be summoned to a hospital where he'll find you fucked-up and traumatised in a guarded cell, only to then go home to collect clean clothes for you and discover that you'd smashed up his house and all of his worldly possessions into pieces and been arrested in front of his neighbours. Poor man. Poor lovely man.

(Then again, you had no idea at that point that he would eventually wish you dead in a text message).

46

Post Complaint //
Wonderful

You are so tired. You are so tired that in your dreams you're
often asleep. You curl up and fall asleep while the action happens all
around you / without you. You are the type of tired that cannot be
cured by sleep but by death and death only. Most of your dreams are
bad ones but last night you dreamt that it was finally the end of the
world. The meteor was coming, getting bigger / louder / closer and
everyone was frantic / frightened / screaming and you had never felt
so calm. It was wonderful. The end of the world was *wonderful*.
The end of the world has given you something to live for.
You look forward to it. You welcome it. You will it.

Post Complaint //
Nevertheless, You Are Left-Handed

Earlier in the day you had an overwhelming urge to chop
your fingers off. Mainly the thumb, index and middle finger of your
left hand.*

You didn't

> [like the feeling of them]

want them

> [attached to you]

at all.

Your skin makes you sick.

You want your skin to stop touching you.

You want your skin to get the hell off of your body.

"GET OFF ME!"

---

* The only thing you do left-handedly is hold a pen to write. You do absolutely
everything else with your right hand. Women used to be burnt at the stake for being
left-handed. You learnt how to roll cigarettes your right-handed father's way and
were taught to use ~~right-handed~~ normal scissors and punch in orthodox stance and
stand on skateboards the way your right-handed brother does. Nevertheless, you are
left-handed. It says so on an official document

you screamed
at your skin

"GETOFFMEGETOFFMEGETTHEFUCKOFFME!"

you screamed
at your skin

repeatedly.

The neighbours probably thought
that the men had come back.

They probably thought, "Oh God, that mad bird
from number 24 is kicking off again."

They probably held

their breath

until

you stopped

trying

to rip

your pretty

ugly

skin off.

Post Complaint //
Blunt Force

You see things and hear things that "aren't real"

> [apparently, according to everybody else
> but it's all real to you]

Your eye keeps twitching; you need magnesium
or potassium

> [you can't remember which and it
> doesn't matter one bit–fuck it,
> let it, let it twitch]

You cannot seem to do crosswords anymore

> [you make mistakes then furiously
> scribble out the whole grid because
> it's ruined]

You turn to books, to literature, believing that
reading will save you

> [when you open your favourite novel,
> the print on the pages don't resemble
> words]

You want to write your sorry little heart out

> [but your words aren't words either and
> you admit that you are a waste of paper]

50

Your brain isn't working properly

     [which makes you incredibly
     angry–your brain is enraged at itself]

You try to slit your incredulity-choked throat

     [and barely make a mark–
     your Daddy's penknife is too blunt]

You try to stab yourself in the stomach

     [your body stops you from creating
     enough force]

You are alive and stupid and angry and your
brain is broken and you are so tired

     [of your brain / body / rage / of being
     tired / of everyone / everything /
     all of it]

Your anti-psychotic medication isn't working, it
doesn't work anymore, it's not working

     ["Well, *obviously*," you say,
     sarcastically, to nobody]

History of Present Complaint //
Twenty-Four & Traumatised

A row of text like the Star Wars opening crawl scrolled on a big screen right behind your eyes, on repeat, in yellow, in white, in gold, bold. The words crawled for a long time, etching themselves onto the bony wall of your skull like a knife dragging across glass. The instructions were clear:

Remove sleeve. Pierce several times.

And it scrolled on and on and on and on and so you did, you removed your sleeve and pierced several times with a paring knife. *STAB! STAB STAB STAB.* The blade bypassed bone, and the knife-point satisfyingly emerged from the underside of your skinny arm: straight through, clean. *Stab stab stab.* How many times is "several" anyway? You didn't stir (the instructions didn't mention anything about stirring halfway through), you just sat still and let yourself marinate in a bloodbath, in your party dress, with sawdust in your hair, and the spider on the wall, and watched the Star Wars crawl gradually fade into no-   thing-   ness.

He found you eventually.

—What the hell are you doing in the attic?

        I can't remem-

—JESUS CHRIST, WHAT HAVE YOU DONE?!

        Well, it said "remove sleeve and pierce several times" so I
        did

—NOT ON YOUR ARM, YOU SILLY COW!

I was just following the instruc-

—YOU ARE NOT A MICROWAVE MEAL!

Sorry, but the-

—YOU ARE NOT A FUCKING LASAGNE!

Every now and then he emails you to remind you that you are not a lasagne.

"I am not a lasagne," you say to yourself when you feel like stabbing.

"I am not a microwaveable meal. I am not a lasagne. I am no longer his. I am not a lasagne. I am not his problem anymore. I am not a lasagne. I am not a lasagne. I am not a fucking lasagne," scrolls on a big screen right behind your eyes, on repeat, in yellow, in white, in gold, bold.

"I am not a fucking lasagne."

Post Complaint //
The Worst Word

You forgot to collect
your veggie pizza

but you cannot forget
receiving that text

shortly after midnight
on January 1st

the one from
the one who

tells you he loves you
the message that said

Fuckin die you slag cunt

and *that* is the worst word
the worst of all the worst words

four letters that make a word so bad that
you cannot bring yourself to say it out loud

so acidic
that even writing it

makes the bile rise
makes your chest hurt

makes you die
an extra death inside

and you do not need to speak it
or even write it because you see it

you see it, you see it all the time, that
four letter word as a bright green neon sign

       puls   ing   erra

tic   ally on

       th   e wall   s of

you   r sku   ll in

      time   wit   h   yo   ur

weak   scat

      ty   litt   le

hea

        rtbe

            at

Post Complaint //
This Business of Living

Listen to me, bub. It's important. I need you to live your life while I try to save my own. If there's one scrap of fight left hiding in me, I will find it, but I am the only one who can. It seems that nobody on earth can help me but, luckily, dead men speak to me regularly. Pavese is keeping me alive tonight, so you don't need to worry. I will see another midnight, but I will see it alone. And until I can conjure one iota of belief in the possibility of recovery and muster some semblance of strength from my broken body (the two things I need to begin the extraordinarily difficult task of rebuilding myself from nothing, again), this is the way that it's got to be. I am sorry, truly, but you have to leave me be. Leave me, and then I'll believe that you love me.

Post Complaint //
Tuesday Triptych

1 /

You keep doing things that are "out of character"

> [you are too many characters]

You have "forgotten how to play the role" of Your Self

> [your brain murdered all of the goodness in you]

"Did you lose the script?"

> [you are full of villains and disasters]

"Have you even bothered to look for it??"

> [you've been typecast / categorised / put in a box]

"Are you sure that such a script even exists???"

> [from now on, you will always be cast as:
>
> the bad / evil / insane one
>
> the waste of [[police]] time
>
> the nightmare
>
> the liar]

2 /

You believe in one for sorrow.

The sight of a solitary magpie

determines your mood

for the rest of the day:

one for sorrow and you are sad.

The superstition ends there.

You do not believe in two for joy.

3 /

On Saturday, it will be three years since your Daddy died.

You read somewhere that once you reach the three-year anniversary of a loved one's passing, the death can no longer be referred to as 'recent.' The death is officially considered as having occurred long enough ago that any grief one may still be feeling can no longer be used to justify typical grief-induced behaviours (angry outbursts, crying in public, actively mourning, the death having a noticeable, significant impact on your daily life, etc.). After the third anniversary, grief can no longer serve as a valid excuse for any of your questionable behaviours or negative emotions.

You are supposed to be "over it" by the third year.

You will never, ever get over it.

You dread the prospect of November.

You are sure that November dreads your arrival, too.

Post Complaint //
The Report

A screenshot of an entry typed in your phone notes

Just read report from Sept.feel sick.trying
not to cry. I lied so good.Too good. I lied
too well. Was i really that convincing?
Apparently so. Sane enough to be released
but that's all i wanted all i wanted was to
getout of that hospitsl. I was born in that
hospital and didn't want to die in there too
like a badly drawn full circle. I scare myself
again and again again i scare myself. What
my brain is capable of is terrifying. To lie
like that to trick the people whose job it is to
see through mind trickery and protect me
they set me free. My illnesses played the
game and won. But i lost. I as a human lost
the game.why didn't they see through my
lies? Why didn't they help me. Why didn't
they see that i was acting for my life for my
freedom. The assessment report described
me as elated laughing embarrassed of the
episode lucid friendl charming cogent
EUTHYMIC fucking euthymic!!!!! I want
to cry.I have a lump in my throat.cant let it
out I can't fall apart now there's no time.
I'm running out of time we are all running
out of time. The badness the bad brain won.
But I   lost. I lost. I lost. I cant cry I don't
have time or spare tears left I can't cry i
can't I can't not now no

History of Present Complaint //
Out of The Mouths of Doctors

The following statements were made directly to the patient by medical professionals and mental health workers in various hospitals in London between 2014 and 2019

Your blood is highly uncooperative.

If you were my daughter, I honestly wouldn't know what to do with you.

I've decided that you are not currently in crisis because you're wearing clean jeans, so you're fine.

Well I guess, going forward, the plan is: keeping taking your meds and try not to kill yourself or anybody else, and we'll reconvene in six months. Sound good?

You have a very shy cervix.

I would let you borrow my pen, but you'll probably steal it.

Either my blood pressure monitor is broken or you're on the cusp of death right now.

Prison might be good for you. Would you be willing to commit a few crimes? You'd get help there, and three meals a day, and then you wouldn't have to worry about housing! It's a win-win for everybody.

It's funny because you look normal.

You can live without water, stop complaining.

Are these from rough sex or do you always bruise like a peach?

Look at the state of you. It's such a shame, you'd be really pretty if you made a bit of effort.

We've run out of vegetarian options, so I've brought you 4 pots of jelly.

Yeah, you don't seem stupid enough to fall pregnant.

You can press this buzzer any time you need help, but please don't press it, it's annoying.

I had a girlfriend like you once. Proper psycho she was. Loved her to bits.

At least when you're mentally ill, life is never boring.

Post Complaint //
Blind (Happy 3rd Death Day Daddy)

My eyes give me away. They are mine but you saw yourself inside them. I see me too: in them, through them, through you. They look so sad, don't they? They betray me. They suit me. They betray me at any opportunity. Sometimes I try to pull my eyes out of their sockets so I can't see any more badness. They stay where they are, stubborn. Full of bad news, kind and wild at the same time. Soft-boiled, just like yours were, but my smiles don't reach them. Bright orange in the sunshine, beached Baltic amber, visions witnessed petrified within. Pinholes when I'm tired or wired or sedated, uninspired. They see too much when they are shut. Incapable of unseeing, deleting, forgetting. The OFF switch is a dud. Even if I gouged them out, I'd forever see you in that bed, your tired chest as it rose and fell for your final breath, your yellow lids, snug over shuttered pupils; if I were to go blind overnight, I'd still see Death holding out his hand for me to take, to shake, and you grabbing it instead, leaving me there so terribly alive, so acutely awake. I would still see these scenes projected on the walls of my chipped-china brain, on repeat, in technicolour, in ultra-HD, on a never-ending loop in such hideous clarity and look, Daddy, LOOK! Look at my eyes now, oh dear, they're running again. My eyes are running again, giving me away again, betraying me again, seeing you again and running again, you in that emaciated state, a shell of a man, and running again and seeing five strange men and the worst word, the evil text message again, and running and seeing all of the badness again, betraying me and running and seeing again and look at them, running, and always seeing everything

Post Complaint //
Dirty Dishes

You're scrubbing at the stain   on the dirty plate

furious   you must make it go away   and you are

more stubborn than it   so although your wrist   is

beginning to ache   and you just felt   your

thumbnail break   you'll stand there   sweating

scouring   for as long as it takes   because you

absolutely *have to*   make this plate perfect   again

and you've worked   yourself up   into a bit of a state

but it's   okay   because   at the end of this   it'll be

beautiful   and you'll have won the game   and so much

time has passed that   your boyfriend   (the owner

of the plate)   comes in to check on you   and he finds

you angry   muttering under your breath

about "this fucking ketchup"   with tears of frustration

spilling down your face   then he says   quietly

"babe, that's not a stain   it's actually   a part of the design

painted on the plate"   and what a terrible revelation   what

a fucking awful thing it is   to learn that no amount   of

soap or force   or sheer determination   will ever fix the plate

to fit your vision   will ever restore it   to your

satisfaction   that its ugliness is permanent its stains   are

there to stay   that in your eyes   it's always going to

be imperfect / tarnished / marred / bloody / imperfect   that

there's nothing   you can do to change   the design of

something that you   didn't create   that no amount of

effort will ever make it   plain again   or   untouched

or pure   or clean   or perfect   or sane again

Post Complaint //
Lovely

You had three nosebleeds today, all
of them highly satisfying, each equally
lovely. The free-falling drop of claret
that lands on your newspaper
at the junction of 21 down and 29
across is such a lovely surprise.
You like to look at the patterns that
the blood paints onto the tissue as if they
were Rorschach inkblots. Bloodblots.
You say what you see because nobody
is beside you to take notes or worry
about what you say that you see (wasps,
exploding grenade, rotten apples,
the Wisła when it flooded, an amphitheatre).
The deciphering of the blots, the eventual stop
as the blood clots. It is so polite of your body
to choose that moment to remind you that
you are alive, when you yourself have
forgotten or weren't entirely convinced.
You roll the tissue between your palms,
moulding the evidence of your existence
into a neat ball, launching it directly
into the bin in the corner, and it lands softly,
a lovely, clean shot. You wipe your nose
with the back of your hand, drag the nib
of the pencil through the blood and now
the answer to 21 down *libel* is written
in red. Snap your head back, set your neck
and dangle your hair over the top edge
of the chair. The taste of rust
as the plasma collects in the crook

of your throat is 29 across:
the clue is 'pleasant, delightful,'
the answer is *lovely*.

Post Complaint //
Things You'll Find When She Dies

Rusty hoop earrings—various sizes. Melted daffodils in a Kronenbourg pint glass. Note that reveals the secret ingredient of her guacamole. 2 x winning scratch-cards. Hunting knife wrapped in a bloody tea towel. One million kirby grips. Punnet of overripe nectarines. 3 x deer skulls. Pile of cigarette ash. Several hundred books. Diet pills. 5 x rabbit skulls. Flutter of coke on a copy of Vogue (Paris, Dec 2015). Rosary blessed by Pope John Paul II. Her Hit-List. Fancy dresses that she'll never get to wear. Emergency £50 note. 1 x Black Ibex horn. Tangle of leggings. Custard-cream crumbs in the bed. Array of plastic carrier bags—various sizes (under the sink). Bowl of rotting "easy peelers" that are *not* easy to peel in the slightest. Shoebox of acrylics, watercolours, inks. Academic records, including her prize-winning essay on poetic energy in William Carlos Williams' *Spring and All* (the one piece of writing she ever asked you to read) (but you didn't). Shrine to her father. Screwdriver under the pillow. Broken Rimmel lipstick (colour #30). Box file containing a lifetime of cards and letters from family, friends and exes. Navy blue 'Proper Cornish' jumper with holes burnt by hash hot-rocks. Enough filled journals to (hopefully) explain her away. Damp box of matches. 4 metres of fake ivy. Freezer that needs defrosting. And finally, a locked wooden box containing The Truth—her truth, and yours, too. The keys are inside the Buddha.

Post Complaint //
And Now You're Doing It

On a whim, you book a one-way ticket to Mexico.
You've always wanted to go there and now you're doing it.
If staying alive is your greatest form of self-harm,
then this trip is the ultimate act of self-care.

Death is a disappearing act.
You think that you'll come back*
but you also think that nothing is ever
certain until it is.

And then, even when you are so fucking certain about something, like
you've never been more certain about anything in all your life,
somebody will call you a liar
and tell you that you're mad.

---

* (that you'll return to London eventually, maybe alive and well with a suitcase full
of tequila, 3000 cheap cigarettes and a renewed sense of Self, possibly inside a body
bag with a slit throat, broken nose and a name tag tied to your toe)

Note To Self //

Hey

> [it was real]
> [they were real]
> [the men]

You were right

> [the men were real]
> [you saw them with your own eyes]
> [they hurt you]

Listen to me

> [you saw them with your eyes]
> [they were real]
> [you didn't lie]

This is important

> [you are not a liar]
> [it was all real]
> [you did not lie]

Whatever you do, don't ever forget what I'm telling you right now

> [it's all real]
> [the men]
> [the men]

You didn't lie

> [they were real]
> [it was all real]
> [it was real]

You are NOT a liar

> [all of the men]
> [all of the badness]
> [all of it was real]

YOU DID NOT LIE

> [your reality was real]
> [you are not a liar]
> [all you have left is
> your truth, your heart
> and the wonderful
> end of the world]

**All you have is your truth, your heart,
and the wonderful end of the world.**

Acknowledgements

◆

History of Present Complaint // Out of The Mouths of Doctors
An earlier version of this was originally published online by *Dear Damsels* [June, 2019]

History of Present Complaint // Twenty-Four & Traumatised
An earlier version of this piece titled *Lasagne* was a winner of The Cambridge Prize for Flash Fiction 2020, a competition hosted by The Short Story. *Lasagne* was published online by *TSS Publishing* [April, 2020]

Post Complaint // Things You'll Find When She Dies
An earlier version of this poem titled *Things You'll Find When I Die* was originally published online by *Anti-Heroin Chic* [February, 2020]

The author would like to thank:
CLD and KR, for their encouragement and belief in me. EW and LE, for their continued kindness and support. AL, for tinned peaches and warmth. SJG and CD, for their patience and hard work. TMR, for absolutely everything. And finally, DC: thank you for you.

About The Author

◆

HLR (she/her) is a writer and editor. She writes poetry and short prose about her real-life experiences with mental illness, grief, and trauma. Her work has been published by *streetcake magazine*, *The Hellebore*, *Constellate Literary Journal*, *Lunate*, *In Parentheses Literary Journal*, *Re-side zine*, *The Daily Drunk*, *Free Verse Revolution*, *Dear Damsels*, *Anti-Heroin Chic*, *Dust Poetry Magazine*, and many others. She lives in north London.

Help & Support

◆

UK:

Samaritans - call 116 123

Shout - text **SHOUT** to 85258

Mind - visit www.mind.org.uk

Talk to Frank – text 82111

USA:

National Suicide Prevention Lifeline - 1-800-273-8255

Crisis Text Line - text **HOME** to 741-741

Information correct at time of printing.

Printed in Great Britain
by Amazon

59220205R00051